Charles Shannon, Charles Ricketts

The Dial

Charles Shannon, Charles Ricketts

The Dial

ISBN/EAN: 9783741199905

Manufactured in Europe, USA, Canada, Australia, Japa

Cover: Foto ©Andreas Hilbeck / pixelio.de

Manufactured and distributed by brebook publishing software
(www.brebook.com)

Charles Shannon, Charles Ricketts

The Dial

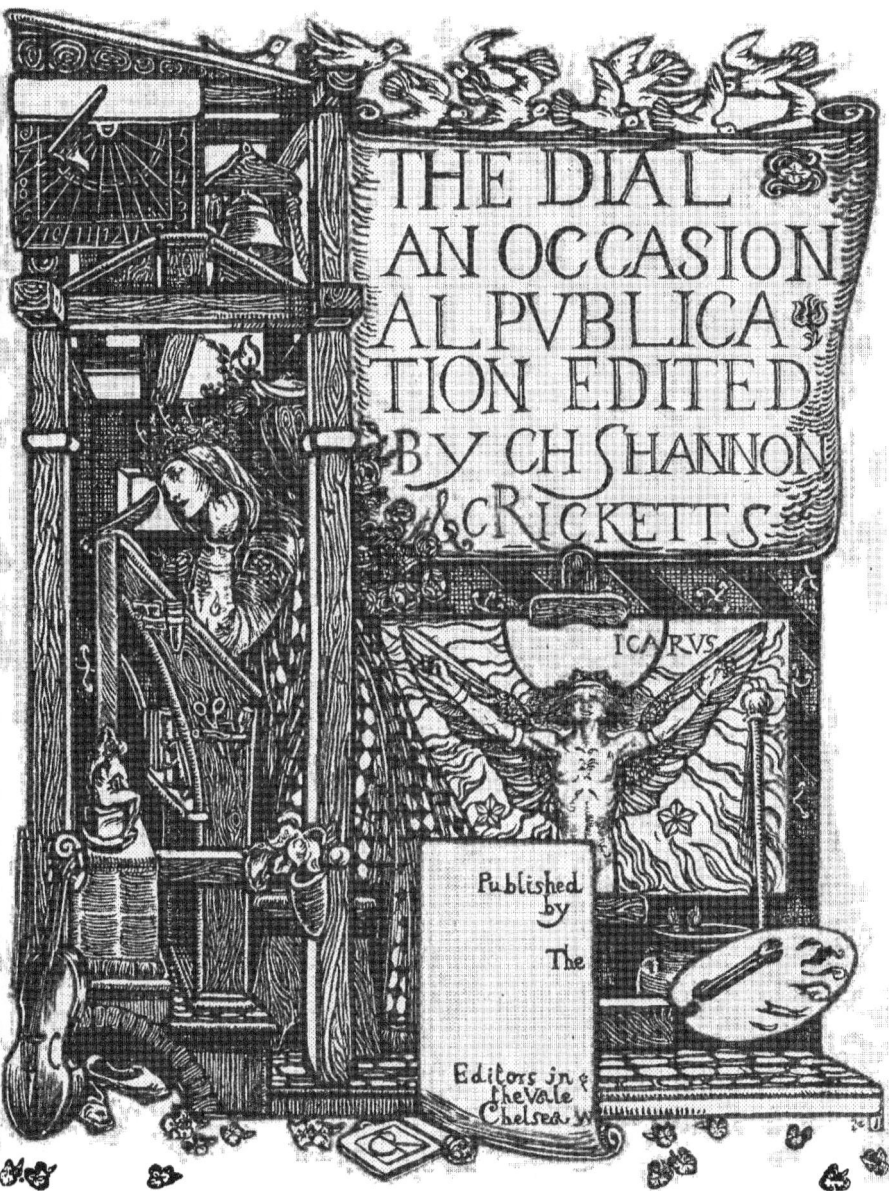

THE DIAL
AN OCCASION
AL PVBLICA
TION EDITED
BY CH SHANNON
& C RICKETTS

ICARVS

Published
by
The

Editors in &
the Vale
Chelsea

⸭   ⸭   ⸭

MY MOUNTAINS ARE MY OWN
AND I WILL KEEP THEM
TO MYSELF
W . BLAKE

I

BOTH city and suburbs re-joiced. From roof to roof-top swayed the bell-like weight of large lanterns that mimicked the languorous airs of lilies on the nod, yet more duskily, like fruit again become blossom, against a faint pink sky still pale with the lingering trail of sunset ; for Chang Tei had laid low that haughty head of his upon Mount Torment, below the prison gates ; and with the dawn of even, when a wan moon-crescent beckoned to clustering stars, and mimic lights from the bridges swam with them in the river, a glow from his still burning house put a dull redness in the air, through which, now and again, shot rapidly a light more acute, when a charred wall crumbled in.

This was watched, long after curfew and into the night, for some beggars sat at a town gate.

The sound of the patrol's retreating footfalls was echoed by overhanging eaves, with this the tremulous expostulations of some belated tippler hurried away ; the night-wind swept past, and the stillness from circling hills sank upon the city.

"Curse me!" quoth beggar Foo, "but Ling must have found a sweet-heart." At this the pent hatred of the others clamoured against those limbs, that whole nose of his: "He a sweetheart forsooth!" They glanced hate-fully at each other's maimed limbs ; as the wind tosses dead tree-branches, so their arms became shaken, for with Ling was their common fund for food. Ah! curse him ; to hide thus from the patrol since sun-down was not pleasant, for the night became cold when the pre-morning wind, that shudders in the chimneys, adds its shriller coolness to the air.

Their hoarse clamour soon spluttered, and gradually ceased ; dull gleams only answered the fixed gleam of hungry eyes ; one idea only troubled their shrivelled lips : then with tacit consent the beggars bent towards the place

1

of Sudden Death, the muffled clank of plodding hand-rests beat a wooden tune to their shadows cast upon the walls they passed.

Some dogs, upon the place of execution, snapped sullenly from right to left, with fangs still clenched in shreds of flesh. Foo was bitten on the hand; at his jarring cry the curs scampered away in a retreat of pattering paws.

About Mount Torment lay what remained, flesh made nameless, then left there by the torturer. One beggar shook from a bamboo stake a head so placed not to be stolen; a silent tussle began for this, in which blows fell upon unelastic shoulders that sounded like bumped wood. In the struggle, this prize had fallen to Foo; his wounded hand still maddened him, and this gave energy to body bent in the effort to propel his little cart; the turning of a few streets soon brought him into security, for the chase had grown slack, a feeble shower of hurled stones ended it.

When he rested to take breath, his hunger had gone, which but now so tormented him. Like an unequal runner, the taste of blood was in his mouth, and he grasped at an oppression near his chest; so he placed the head upon the ground, for it had grown heavy.

Something, as yet but half understood, flashed suddenly upon him, as if an oblique light, full of revelation, had been cast between his eyes and the dead man's eyes; vanishing, it left a partial recollection, or echo, in his brain, vibrant as a splash of white upon a ground of black, but, like it, formless.

When, gradually, colour upon colour, the past, unrolled, swam upon the filmy web, many things came back unbidden, as if, in sleep, he walked some ominous strand girt with the refluent sweep of persistent recollection, repeating—

" Do you remember, do you remember?" the dead man's eyes added, " You left by the wrong gate, I lost you in the garden; I, Chang Tei, have hated her, ever since "—" ever since," whispered the little memories,
" Ever since ! "

Now, Foo understood why the night-watch had seized him beyond the gate—as a robber? or conspirator? he had never known; things had been wrenched from him, groaned in excess of anguish, when blinded by torture; things whose purport he had not then understood.

Though no kinsman dared succour him, he had escaped; ten years had passed since the paying of her kisses with his blood.

For hours the silent dialogue continued between the dead man and the maimed.

Dawn tinged a summer pavilion near the royal orchards, when the beggar again reached the terrible Present, with its livid light that streaked the opposite walls, as with the stain of tears.

A lamp-ray shot from a lattice, for a moment opened; the sound of trailed viol strings floated past with the projected glimmer.

Then, he remembered the time and place; taking the head, he hurled it through the unclosed window.

The marred face fell upon the queen's lap; when she rose with suddenly clenched eyelids, she felt its weight bite into her robe.

No one stirrred, their terror had not passed ; from a word gasped by a servant, her casual lover knew his mistress was the queen ; he dared not move whilst her eyes remained shut.

Her teeth clattered, and from the throat came forth a shuddering sound, as of something unwound slowly.

The fatal head merely looked at her ; between its eyes and hers, one recollection had grown, at first impalpably, but gradually, with such oppression that she opened them wide and closed her hands convulsed.

" Water ! give me wine ! "

A great silence fell. She became aware that her lips moved inaudibly.

A sense of void, that yet seemed conscious with a threat and terribly near, hung upon her. Had the world slipped away, out of time's control? and the idea of calling for assistance seemed so absurd.

Of its own accord the head rolled over. Once more she gurgled from the throat, with short, hurt moans, and leant over the dead face, as if dragged there perforce ; in rapid succession came the remembered sensation of a jostling palanquin, some women beckoning from a balcony, and a great sense of fear that made her remember his name : but the angle of a villa swam past in moonlight ; with it the sensation of a nestling kiss ; she remembered the rest, and became conscious.

She feared the attendants heard these certain things, and motioned unsteadily to them to go, to leave the room ; and all this had taken but a little while, for the wine still flowed from the gullet of a fallen jar, it ceased with a loud " Sob " ; remembering her lover's presence, she saw his face was frightful ; with a terrified murmur she said " Go away " !—he turned and left very suddenly.

Birds inaudible by day made the air acute with bleeding sounds, pulsed from red throats unassuaged. Above the lawns, the morning mists hung loose a silvery green which clung about and tinged the lower tree-trunks.

When the queen, with dull, relaxed eyelids, gazed through the window, the summer pavilions without seemed diminutive in the morning light, as if shrunken in the new sense of air, of space ; the room was no longer doubly stained by blended dawn and lamp haze, the lamp had gone out.

She felt stunned with all that face had said to her, from the time that a hesitating blueness had been let in with the opening of a shutter, to the Now that filled the walls with a diffused radiance that bleached the lattice ; those lips had mumbled all their hatred, explaining, accusing and repeating ; then, haggard images faced her on all sides, peopling many mirrors that circled or ceiled the love chamber,—might they not mirror the marred face ? This gave her strength to rise, and fold it in her robe ; she would take it to the river.—Several times she pushed the head from the shore, for the river there seemed without current ; heedless of her efforts, his lips smiled, as if they sketched a kiss in the air and said " why do you try? you cannot do this thing."

When Summer came, and the days brooded and grew still, beneath a sky that drooped, a glance of his would cling to her, his voice remembered would

3

seem Time's central voice, heard only at intervals ; sometimes it sobbed, like
the river beyond the gardens, whilst the fountains tall beat time without and
dreamt they touched the eaves.—" You did not know that we should meet
so soon? but see!"—she even heard this after having locked the head in a
box ; and sometimes a mirror remembered his face ; she had this covered
up, never returning to that part of the palace. People said these mirrors
were covered because the queen was daily losing her beauty ; there was some
truth in this ; her dead lover haunted her with unforgiving eyes, only the
more implacable when she closed hers to the light ; and, through this terrible
obsession, the ghost of another feeling would sometimes steal upon her and
make still, for a second only, the unrelenting fierceness with which his eye-
balls looked at her ; then she would cry, in pity of herself.

Once his face had looked at her from the burnished gilding of an
oratory, where she had gone to complain. Her pride was broken. If, at
times, her old haughtiness returned, and, with it, deep gusts of wantonness,
she found terror painted upon love's face ; some occasional lovers had even
to be executed, for they had talked ; those were such troubled times. Their
death seemed to her useless, foolish, but the laws of the country forbade
the slandering of the queen.

Slowly, she sank into a torpor, vague, but almost delightful ; she dreamt
of shadeful places, deep with boughs, long murmurous grasses,—places where
the large flowers seemed mellow sounds,—and that his glance had there
grown still. A belief in this would flow through her limbs with a soft,
velvety sensation.

Gradually, in these hallucinations, the dead man's voice whispered
gently, in tones that till then had been forgotten ; and the newer sound
would swell within her, like the long sun-streaks that glow and fade across
a stretch of famished grass. Thus, something of the waning summer's
pleasantness sank into her life, as it grew more and more unreal and blent
with the moods of the sleeping palace, giving moment to the yawn of a
curtain gently swayed by the breeze, the shimmer from the floors, their
clinging coolness poured beneath the cedar beams that cracked and stretched ;
those things that give the sense of the hours as they fall from the hands of
time like the beads from a chaplet ; till once, in very sooth his voice did
call from the sealed and spiced box in which she had placed this dead face
to embalm.

Like one in a trance she rose to go to him.

But the head rolled over with a branding peal of laughter ; exasperated,
she struck it passionately, again and again, till her hands were wet with tears
—great tears streamed from his eyes ; and her bowels yearned, as thick
drops gathered about her lashes, that she could have done this thing! she
kissed him, and they wept together.

Facing the queen was a picture she had often, if but vaguely, noted ;
rich with age, as with clinging incense haze, the painted figure was clothed
in a violet robe that curved outwardly ; it held a tongueless bell in one hand,
the other rose to close its laboured lips ; the eyes were fixed unfathomably
into space, they got their strangeness by the rigid distinctness with which

4

the artist had pencilled them—those eyes seemed to have grown pallid in the effort to forget.

Through her clustering tears she suddenly remembered the picture ; the resemblance of its lips to those of her lover broke upon her like a sudden bell-sound heard in the centre of a wood. The painting had been called "Silence"; some said it represented Fate: beneath the queen's kisses Chang Tei very slowly closed his eyes.

Time passed, the summer days returned ; legends about the queen took clearer, if still fragmentary form ; she was of alien blood, remotely of Tartar origin. During the disturbances the Chang Tei rebellion had left in the larger towns, those voices had grown louder that sing little, forbidden songs, or give vent to exclamations in an amused crowd.

Some things were coarse and cruel, their infamy delightful to those who could best understand it. When a few are gathered together, will not a song give, sometimes, to the singer a flattering sense of nationality ?—some originality of feeling steals unawares through a chorus not sung too loud, but to which people nod pleasantly as they go by the half-closed door.

There were other things, however, not to be understood ; the queen's poignant passions, this one supreme renunciation seemed only able to assuage—how unaccountable this ! She used to terrify her lovers, about this there were many ingenious tales. Now, it was said she would wash this marred face with her tears, wipe, devoutly, with her hair, the precious ointments she poured upon its many wounds, kissing the spiced mouth ; she was as one who has listened to much prolonged music, or who half fears the approach of a vision.

And men, with shrill voices, said a curse was upon her for her lewdness ; that an iron circle weighed upon her brow from nightrise to sunrise, but that her lover had no cause to fear, being but a face ; and people would laugh exceedingly at this ; also, was that Face not deeply marred ?

Though trouble, ever increasing, raged in the provinces, the queen's life did not change ; none but a few servants who had seen the head's coming had access to her.

In long rooms, hung with violet veils, or dark bronze mirrors filled only with a remote radiance, she nightly feasted with him, raising empty goblets to her lips, breaking untasted bread sacramentally ;—though a banquet was laid nightly, she tasted but a little rice. When morning came she would motion towards a window and say, " My Lord ! the Dawn breaks." Rising, she would bear the head in her hands, devoutly, as a young priest does a relic, through darkened corridors, where the purple shapes seemed absorbed in the recreating of forms half remembered, of colours half effaced ; and she would murmur the while quaint foolish songs she had learnt in her youth.

And behold ! rebellion stood boldly at the gates of her capital with a rejoicing populace issuing thence with appropriate presents, whilst in the queen's house all was still, as a place the south wind has swept over and left withered.

News reached the palace; the servants issued from lateral gates; they looked sharply about them as if to see if it rained, dropping ostentatiously their long lances, or feathered brooms, if any one chanced to be near; but as yet no crowd circled the many royal buildings. Here and there stood a few men only, who blinked somewhat at the light, and watched, quietly, as birds watch a dying traveller. Some amongst them swung long arms, with hooked hands a little distance from their sides, scarcely knowing what to do with them.

When the sudden crowd came with the Deliverers beating their drums, the imperial peacocks and other birds flew, clamouring, into the air to perch on unaccustomed roof projections and pinnacles. A deaf old servant came out after this noise; crossing the main drawbridge, he held one hand to his ear as if to listen. At this the crowd laughed merrily.

Room after room was crossed, in good order as yet, with a little laughter only when there was no exit, and the same rooms had to be crossed again.

In the halls, the many paintings looked at the crowd; some represented princes battling with waves or waterfalls; ladies among peonies; there were pictures of gentle beasts, preciously wrought; portraits of beautiful Empresses,—one had been covered with a dish-clout, for her servants, wishing to conceal the picture, had not dared destroy it, not knowing the town would open all its gates to the insurgents, so many things might have happened. The crowd by this time a little awed again laughed, then moved on.

At last a cry of rage broke from them all; the queen could nowhere be found. Some among the rebels said the carved figures on a roof represented all the sins, that the topmost figure, tulip-shaped, was an image of sterility; at any rate the splendours of this temple roof maddened them,—had it not been built with what might have been in each man's larder? And the prince, of royal Chinese descent, who had headed the crowd, borne in a long litter, made a sign with his hands; his followers knew he wished nothing to remain of this palace, builded by an alien dynasty, and torches became spontaneous in the crowd.

The noise, which had hitherto filled the fantastic palace pavilions, ceased, even without, and an oppressive lull swept heavily through the open doors, and thence into the gardens.

On the lawns the birds had settled again, but once more they twisted their necks and bent their legs as if for flight; the Royal Tigers walked up and down their cages, or, lifting their front paws, they snuffed the air, as cats do at a scented flower they do not think they like; white hares shot from cover to cover and listened. No smoke was as yet visible—but a thin crackling sound disturbed them.

When lithe flames bent from some windows, the alarm scarcely increased; the birds strutted about or took little foolish flights; out of the bamboo stubble came the quaint squeak of the quail, the flutter of partridges.

Upon the walls, large painted spaces retained their surface colour unto the last, between the bursting and licking of the flames. Creeping plants writhed from heated bricks. The clatter of tiles sliding away to where their

6

fall was no longer heard came, repeatedly, from a portion of the palace now a widening flame.

A flight of peacocks wheeled round and round, as they fell, suffocated, into the fire. The great sullen Behemoth then broke from his tank, in which he loves to wallow in ooze and mire ; first among the beasts he had snuffed, but had not moved, he had rolled little red eyes long before the outbursting of the flames. When, indeed, the heat grew terrible, he ran with his snout low down, hurling out of existence beasts that stood in his path, to beat against a part of the palace not yet on fire.

After the garden fountains had ceased, and their water had grown choked and turbid with fallen sparks, all the animals howled with a terrible voice that had a blare as of brass, echoing to the very innermost room, where the queen sat beneath the picture of Silence.

The palace burns, and Behemoth ! but in her ears the roar was faint as the booming of a neighbouring sea, as the fall of land down some hill-slope.

Slowly, but very slowly, some smoke drifted between those walls that were covered with burnished bronze.

"Love!" she said, "I think the dawn has come! for there is a redness in the air, love! see, the morning mist is on the floor, filtered to this room." She laughed quietly, remembering it was still day, not even twilight, for no servant had come, and without them she knew not, nor troubled to know, how the spent hours waned.

Then it seemed to her the palace burned, as a little sound like a mouse crept among the hangings that smouldered duskily, near the chink of a bronze door ; and the mist was filmy with smoke.

She knew that, owing to the gold upon them and the silver woven in their web, the curtains could scarcely burn ; the burnished walls and finished floors were covered with bronze plating ; heat only, and suffocation, could overtake her.

"My love," she said, "the palace burns, let us go away." Donning a fastidious robe, entirely radiant with wings outstretched upon its tissue, she nodded to him and sang vaguely, unwound her hair and painted her eyes, that he might be proud of her beauty ; they would go away, the palace burned, the gods were so envious.

Door after door was crossed and left behind ; the muffled rooms burnt noiselessly, each sinking into *A past* as she walked to meet the future. Her dilated eyes caught glimpses of the whiteness of her skin, the morsels of beauty that remained to her ; the black mirrors had veiled the ageing of her face.

Some of the insurgents saw her glide above a tall, smooth wall that led to a disused pavilion near the palace orchards, the culminant fire behind her as a frame. The fixity of her gaze was centred on the dead man's eyes.

Some one in the crowd hurled a javelin that stuck into a door before her. But still she kissed her lover's face, as if she inhaled the deep fragrance of a flower. Then, as the pavilion had no outer door, as she could go no further, she reverentially kissed his marred face before them all.

Some say that owing to her great sinfulness she sang a wanton song.

7

PARSIFAL.

IMITATED FROM THE FRENCH OF PAUL VERLAINE.

Conquered the flower maidens, and the wide embrace
Of their round proffered arms that tempt the virgin boy :
Conquered the trickling of their babbling tongues ; the coy
Back glances ; and the mobile breasts of supple grace.

Conquered the WOMAN BEAUTIFUL ; the fatal charm
Of her hot breast ; the music of her babbling tongue :
Conquered the gate of Hell ; into the gate the young
Man passes, with the heavy trophy at his arm—

The holy javelin that pierced the Heart of God.
He heals the dying king ; he sits upon the throne,
King ; and high priest of that great gift the living Blood.

In robe of gold the youth adores the glorious Sign
Of the green goblet ; worships the mysterious Wine.
And o, the chime of children's voices in the dome !

JOHN GRAY.

8

TO THE FLOWERS, TO WEEP.

Weep, roses, weep ; and straightway shed
    Your purest tears.
Weep, honeysuckles, white and red :
And with you, all those country dears ;

Violets, and every bud of blue,
    More blue than skies ;
Pinks, cowslips, jasmines, lilies too,
    Pansies and peonies.

For she, that is the Queen of flowers,
    Though called the least,
Lies drooping beneath dreadful Hours,
Megaera has from Hell released.

Weep, till your lovely heads are bent :
    Weep, you, that fill
The meadow-corners ; and frequent
All the green margins of the rill.

Flood, flood your cups with crystal tears,
    Until each leaf,
Each flower, through all the upland, wears
The dole and brilliance of your grief.

So that the Lark, who had from heaven withdrawn,
    Re-sing to you
His song, mistaking noon for dawn,
    And those your tears for dew.

HERBERT P. HORNE.

TO THE MEMORY OF ARTHUR RIMBAUD.

Thou sprung of warrior loins amid hill shade,
A wind-like variance maketh odd thy life,
With wild adventure rife.
Thy child's-feet, racing with thy thoughts unstaid
By fagging flesh, then won thee wider scope,
To fly thy kite of hope,
Than childhood can command.   " All breaths are laid ;
Flints glare ; how far all birds and springs appear.
Hush ! draws the world's end near."
Thy wondrous virile youth all Europe made
An unfenced hunting-park ; its every tongue
Speaking, thou yet wert young :
And sun-got children met thee down each glade
—Familiar god or goddess—gave thy days
A memorable face.
Yet she by all who fashion forms obeyed,
To whom the waves give birth eternally,
Alone was wooed by thee.
Fate-filled thy friendships were ; and it is said,
Like Marlowe, forebear of heroic verse,
Thou wert where women curse,
And in a broil his price had all but paid.
Once manhood reached, world-wide became thy range
In search of new and strange.
The rumours of thy progress hardly fade
On those shores named by waves no vessels ride ;
And sun-scorched sand-seas wide,
Are haunted by suspicion thou hast strayed
O'er them.   For thou rov'dst like thy losel boat,
Which tenantless did float
Past monumental dreams on shores displayed
(Down world-long rivers) till dissolved by these
And drunk up by deep seas ;
It, like thee, o'er their aspects sovereign swayed.

T. Sturge Moore.

ERTAIN mansions in Art's home, without being wealthy, splendid, magisterial or of god-gauged proportions, though not always without, have a quality of apartness strangely attractive. When the afternoon mist gnaws the hill-hollow leech-like, till it become cavitous in the twilight, and the head and shoulders of the mountain hang—like the gorgeous roof of a crystal palace—above receding halls of quietude, vaguely visible through the vapour-veil (transparent to the eye of Turner, that man who scaled heaven every week-day, and on Sundays went to Wapping; to other eyes but tantalizingly suggestive of discovery); there, or, as Swinburne sings,
"Here, where the world is quiet,"
by the hearth of a mind, when the evensong dies down, Memory is a mother, Passion a soulless woman of perfect charm, and, quite separate from her, Love like a sister or dear friend clothed and in her right mind: there too Mystery moves a maiden, Awe is a child, and Fear impossible.

Such is the aspect of mind or mountain not unfitly to be termed holy—but for the narrow and squalid daily application of the word—which is found from time to time the only, the chief or one of the decorations of a room in our Lady's House.

To me especially certain works, singly or collectively, of a few artists seem to be the produce of such holy seclusion, not from the world, but in it: the preface of Boccaccio's Decameron, with its sweet all-fatherly benignity; Dante's Vita Nuova, the conceited, imaginative masque of love and attendant sorrows.

To Chérie, the tragedy of love-starved maidenhood, De Goncourt has imparted something of the parental tenderness of the old Italian; while Rossetti's House of Life has more than surpassed, at least in scope, the old love-drama.

Other names might be added, other works particularized. I do not attempt that completeness of criticism, necessarily futile, which leaves nought unsaid : striving merely to give form to my own impression on reading the work of De Guérin ; ascribing to him the quality I have attempted to single out from among the rich dowries of the masters.

The clatter of centaur heels has not the harsh factual ring of realism, yet is perfectly whole in life-likeness; though separated by the immense fog of time's breath, palpable in the cold embrace of space, from our ears.

"The rumbling of my going is more beautiful than the plaints of woods, than the noise of water."

When, cooled by night's exhalation of day's sweat, he in the mouth of the cavern hears the inarticulate sleep-speech of the earth mother,—

"Then the foreign life, that had penetrated me during the day, detached itself drop by drop, returning to the peaceful bosom of Cybele; as, after the shower, the remnants of the rain attached to the leafage have their fall and rejoin the runnels."

"At times, when watching in the caverns, I have believed that I was about to overhear the dreams of the sleeping Cybele; and that the mother of gods, betrayed by sleep, was babbling secrets: but I have never recognized aught but sounds which dissolved in the breath of the night, or words inarticulate as the bubbling hum of rivers."

When his mother returns with material memories of the Unknown fresh on her body,—

"My growing-up was almost entirely in the shades where I was born. My abode was buried at such a depth in the thickness of the mountains, that I should have been ignorant of the side of issue, if, turning astray sometimes in at this opening, the winds had not driven there freshets of air and sudden troubles. Sometimes also my mother returned, surrounded with the perfume of valleys, or dripping from waves she frequented. And, these incomings she made without ever instructing me of valleys or rivers, but followed by their emanations, disquieting my spirits, I roved to and fro agitated in my shades. 'What are they," I said to myself, 'these withouts, to which my mother betakes herself, and in which reigns something of such power that it calls her to it so frequently?'"

When, turning, he views his flanks' labour,—

"Thus, while my agitated flanks possessed the inebriation of the course, above them I relished its pride, and turning my head, I stayed myself some time to consider my smoking crupper."

When arrested in full gallop by imminent approach to the Unseen,—

"In the midst of the most violent courses, it has happened to me suddenly to break off my gallop, as if an abyss yawned up to my feet, or a god stood upright before me."

Pervading these passages is the home-feeling of such rooms as reveal Art housewifely. This sense within the sense is not perhaps the grandest quality for the artist; yet is it not one of the rarest? and to it is here added beauty of detailed—especially of landscape—description, as, in The Bacchante, of the wind-cradled birds.

"When they, obeying the shades, lower their flight towards the forests, their feet stay themselves against branches, which, piercing into the sky, are easily rocked by gusts which pass across the night.

For even into their sleep they revel in the seizure of the wind; and like

Many, probably, may here stop, surprised to find freshly handled, work already once finished and signed by Matthew Arnold. He, in remodelling each sentence, seems not only to become a distinct but a distant echo. "What is it,' I cried, 'this outside world whither my mother is borne, &c.,'" this is not literal, and tastes ready made to my palate; as does not the piquant personal use of the word "dehors" as exceptional in French as its literal transcript in English.

their plumage to shiver and dispart at the least breaths that come upon the top of the woods."

After a day which the warm wine of Bacchus has made drowsy,—

"The birds lifted themselves above the woods, searching the sky, if the going of the winds is re-established ; but, still drunken, their wings barely furnished a rickety flight full of error."

A marvel too this latter work ; though not approaching The Centaur in realization, yet has it, and perhaps on this account, a more unbridled sympathy with the moodiness of Nature melting Maenad mountain and moving sea into a common existence.

"Sometimes from the hesitation of her steps, seeking assurance, and from the air of her head, constrained and laden, one had said she walked at the bottom of the ocean."

"When I stayed my feet on the highest of the hills, I shook like the statues of the gods in the arms of priests who lift them up to the sacred pedestals."

This oneness with Nature was his as a little lad, when the wind went through him, standing under, as through the branches bending over, and drew from both an adequate expression.

"Oh ! how beautiful they are, those noises of Nature, those noises abroad in the airs, which rise with the sun and follow him ; follow the sun as a grand concert follows a king.

Those noises of waters, of winds, of woods, of hills, of valleys ; the rollings of thunders and of globes in space ; magnificent noises, with which are mixed the finer voices of birds and of thousands of chanting beings. At each step, under each leaf, is a little violin.

Oh ! how beautiful they are, those noises of Nature, those noises abroad in the airs.

How full of them are the days of summer ! What resoundings, when the plains burst into life and joy like big grown-up girls ; when from all sides rise laughter and songs ; the cadence of flails through the air, with the accompaniment of crickets . . . . and those harmonious and inexpressible breaths that are without doubt the guardian angels of the fields ; those angels who have for hair the rays of the sun.

Oh ! how beautiful they are, those noises of Nature, those noises abroad in the airs."

Of the man, author of these few pages where one scents, plucked in Mnemosyne's hand, flowers which bloomed nigh two thousand years ago, finding them just as sweet as to-day's with this difference, the pungency of immortality, we know all that is ever known of the dead, friends' opinions, letters, journal, and all, to the least facts of his life, uninteresting, apparently unimportant, except as fetters. Many, whom his work attracts, by its freedom from the cloying of modern circumstance so pitifully visible even in the best work, would turn in disgust from the man, never freed entirely from a repulsive Christianity, to which his nature was antipathetic. His journal and letters are, however, enlivened by draughtsmanlike sketches of landscape, though burdened by much soul-questioning, doubting and obduracy of dogmatic faith.

13

Among his most famous critics have been Georges Sand, Sainte-Beuve and Matthew Arnold. The first wrote him a worthy panegyric, by way of introduction to fame: with the two latter, however much we may admire their characters as men, the foolish notion of immaculate criticism blights all freshness of individual sympathy, or nearly all, in their work; both seem chiefly engrossed with the capacity for wear presented by the cloak of accident, which in this case proves too heavy for the spirit-fire and ends by smothering it.

Matthew Arnold, when he leaves the man for the essential artist, compares him to Keats; which comparison seems to me inapt. De Guérin had none of the splendid virility and spontaneity of Keats; Keats had not De Guérin's exquisite taste and next to perfect finish. Keats is ardent, creative, curious; De Guérin reflective, analytical, nice. They have in common delicate susceptibility,—a small link to chain the frank revelry of the Englishman to the composed reserve of the Frenchman.

To my mind the work presenting the closest English equivalent to De Guérin's is the Marius of Pater, though wider in scope, more difficult of execution, and less evidently perfect in realization ; there is a staid mannerliness in their treatment, and a ruminant delectation of after-thought, so at variance with Keats's masterly relish of attainment, which to the manly might of his impetuosity appeared always discovery.

He said, "If a sparrow come before my window, I take part in its existence and pick about the gravel." How different the "Toutes choses mieux ressenties que senties" of De Guérin ; whose nature, if not ample like that of Keats, is rare, refined, a thing set apart for the delight of separate natures, lulling them into the reflective mood of long interminable summer afternoons, the indolent mental season of mature comprehensive possession !

14

ON A PICTURE BY PUVIS DE CHAVANNES.

A spacious land lies large in broad daylight ;
    A warm wind healthily goes to and fro,
    As a dear woman here might come and go ;
In courtesy the trees incline their height,
Rustling their robes as folk at a wedding might ;
    And full of flowers the grass, by scythes laid low,
    Scents the sunshine, while peeps the weak willow
Into pride's paradise in waters bright.

A patriarchal people dwell in peace
And plenty perfect without wealth's increase ;
    Nursed in the lap of lowland hills, their homes
Are gay with flowers ; both morn and evening airs
Are guests within their doors ; and for their prayers
    Cows safely calve, bees build big honeycombs.

BITTEN APPLES.

Their couch the pliant strength of lusty grass,
Cool shade of leaves their canopy, "Alas,"
Sing many maidens, crouched upon their knees
Or lain full-length among the flowers for ease,
                    " Alas, how slow, how slow,
                      Time's hobby-horse does go."

Some hold their hands above their heads, to touch
And handle—Eve-forgetting—fruit, so much
Their cheeks' colour yet cool unlike their cheeks.
Their taste-stung tongues still tell, how " Every week's
                    A week of weeks ; so slow
                    Time's hobby-horse can go."

To idle hearts the day is weariness,
And to lax limbs the land heart's heaviness ;
For all their hearts are healed : long time ago
Hunter Love satisfied hung up his bow.
                    Their song dies down as slow
                    As Time's play-horse can go.

15

LOVE LIES BLEEDING.

SONG FROM A FAIRY TALE.

Love lies bleeding,
Fevers feeding
On flesh which swords have stricken.
Should sweet blood clot and thicken?
How could they slay him so,
When were pleading
Such eyes as his, you know?

                Such eyes, such woe !

THE LITTLE BROWN WOOD-MOUSE.

A little brown wood-mouse
His ample fur cloak doffed,
Then tied his comforter
Before he left the house ;
'Twas lamb's wool, bleached and soft.
To see his tail was there,
   He turned his head ;
   Then off he sped,
To look if beech-nuts were
   Silver or red.

GUST-DISGUSTED GEESE.

The sun makes dust on the highways ;
   The wind pokes fun at the geese ;
With feathers blown all sideways,
   In walking they find no ease.

Let them spread wings, in it rushes,
   As though to bulge out a sail ;
Away they're blown, on the bushes
   To wreck like yawls in a gale.

LES CHERCHEUSES DE POUX.

AFTER ARTHUR RIMBAUD.

When, forehead full of torments hot and red,
The child invokes white crowds of hazy dreams,
Two sisters tall and sweet draw near his bed,
Whose fingers frail nails tip with silv'ry gleams.

The child before a window open wide,
Where blue air bathes a maze of flowers, they sit ;
And in his heavy hair dew falls, while glide
Their fingers terrible with charm through it.

So hears he sing their breath which dread hush curbs ;
How rich with rose and leafy sweets it is !
It sometimes a salival lisp disturbs
On th' lip drawn back, or deep desires to kiss.

Through perfumed silences their lashes black
Beat slow ; from soft electric fingers he,
In colourless grey indolence, hears crack
'Neath tyrant nails the death of each small flea.

Then wells in him the wine of idleness,
Delirious power, the harmonica's soft sigh :
The child still feels to their long drawn caress
Ceaselessly heave and swoon a wish to cry.

17

PYGMALION.

To work at sunrise nor till sunset rest,
　　Week's end spliced in week's end : 'twas thus he wrought ;
　　Tools blunt,—not patience tempered by hot thought.
With eager bare arms leant across her breast
He chiselled chin or cheek, and, where they pressed,
　　His labour's sweat made bright the marble bust.
　　At length she stands amid the workshop dust
In proudest pose of loveliness undressed.

His work once stayed, he, weakened by long strife,
Falls like a swathe from summer-heat's keen scythe :
　　So sees he, waking at the day's decease,—
Not the sea-mothered mother of all life,
　　Then vanished—but alone, alive he sees
　　A naked woman quailing at the knees.

ON A DRAWING BY C. H. S.

Deep-noted thy bucolic peace,
　　Such as no rose-lured insect hum
Or witty water-splash can tease ;
　　In staid divine delirium
　　Entranced till princely Palma come.

　　　　　　　　　　T. Sturge Moore.

18

ATHERED together on the lea-slopes, trees jostle elbows in sheer jolliness; wind makes cornfields heave in waves, like the sunny locks spread over a little girl's shoulders, who on the nursery floor lies laughing over her Nonsense Book; and blue skies grow jealous of the rival beauty of many streams, which gladden that land where stands, under steep tile roofs, the red-brick, slit-windowed, tall-towered castle of King Comfort.

This fortress was never even shaken by fierce assault or battery's bluff bluster; first, because the mortar its walls were built with had been welded with dragon's blood; secondly, as no one ever made attack or fired cannon against its walls.

On its blue bosom a moat bore water-lilies beneath the ladies' bower; and not infrequently apple-parings, crayfish claws, and other refuse swam on its shadow-blackened surface under the scullery-grate.

"Creak, creak," went the well-winder, while chain and pail rattled down to the depths; the groom, scratching his poll, stood and watched pigeons, whose nerves, never wrung with headache, give not the least start at the harsh cry of the iron; which stopped, he ejaculates "I'll swill ditch slush rather than believe but what the king lives," then bends his back and lengthens his arms as he labours at the now weighted handle. But when the bucket arrived at the top, mopping himself, he groaned out "By all the wool-spools my mother's spun, bless her heart, I'm as sure as that crabs are less sweet than pippins that good old Comfort's stone dead."

Then, the stable-lad flung the kennel doors open, and bulldogs, beagles, harriers, spaniels, retrievers, black, piebald, fox-coloured, milk-splashed, rush yelping, barking, and bounding into the court, while the pigeons wheel into the air; a great mastiff oversets the newly drawn water.

What Gunter said after the second descent of the pail, cannot be recorded; for it was more fit to have issued forth from the gargoyles, which yawned, like griffins, devils, belial-men, and bishops, round the roof, while swallows built nests between their rumps and the coping.

Prince Pleasaunce, straddling his legs as wide as the arch of a stone

19

bridge, stood in breeches of tan kid, which sprung, like sturdy oak saplings, from green velvet shoes gashed with white puffs; his coat, lined with fox-fur, hung open to the knees, within it a saffron doublet crossed by a maze of straps shining with buckles, to which hung his hunting-horn, knives, and wallets; he held between his teeth the lithe end of a dog-lash, while the short handle, made from a hart's foot, swung among a litter of boar-hound pups; they frisked, gambolled, and tumbled together in attempts to seize it, while their mother blinked at them from the sunlight that streamed through the hall-windows, over the head of his cousin Gascoigne.

Who, legs out-thrust, lounged on a settle, dressed scarcely less gaily than the other (capped with grey blue satin, a black plume of cock's feathers a-top), now and again grabbing at motes which spun in the large rays above.

"'Say, Pleassy, I don't mind waging a sly couple of cousin Nell's kisses, the old boy's heart's cold, that is to say, you're king, lad." Presently, receiving no answer from his pup-engrossed cousin, he got up; strolled out over the drawbridge, then round by the moat, till he was under the bower-lattice; flopped down on the bank; and began to throw small stones in the moat, striking up at the same time a roundelay. In a few moments a display of wonderful caps flowered out from the windows, and showerlike little laughs, "Good morning, cousin," "Holiday health to Sir Gascoigne," "A merry matin," "Fine day, Sir," "Hope ye quit bed the right side," and like pleasant phrases dropt in the grass all round.

"Is poor Leonine's foot healed?"

"O, don't bother about dogs! I can't bear them, they always smell fusty."

"O, how can you! not when they're kept sweet."

"No, indeed, my sweet mistresses; there's many a gallant, I assure you, prefers his dogs to the ladies, though, in my opinion, with loss thereby of right to the title."

"Ah! they rank equally with you."

"No! now give me a chance; I'd swop a whole pack against any of your neat selves."

"Oh! oh! flattery."

"Does one of my witching queens know whether the king, haply, yet lives?"

All the girl-flowers vanish instantly; presently one only returns with "Hush, you must not shout so; but this moment there was light along the gallery, and the king's daughter walked."

"Ah, you lazy lout, stealing the dripping! There you go, slobberin' it on your face!—Body of me! if thou wasn't such a wain-load, I'd ha' caught the knave, and lugged his ear for 'im,—them boys's always got their lips to sucking something they'd no right touch.—Bless my puckered thumbs! what's a' that? Lor! beg pardon, I'm sure, sir, but your black hat is that tall,—well it just be nothing more nor less than a witch's steeple."

"Good cook, have no fears. I come from my prince, commissioned to add a wee pinch of spice, some little tit-bit, dainty morsel, or as the French

put it ' bonne bouche,' to the apple charlotte I hear you have prepared so skil-
fully for the daughter of our royal master."

"O, sir, it's no great matter to make a charlotte; I've done billions on
'em in my time.—Well I I wouldn't have thought that white powder 'ld make
mickle difference; looks just like sugar."

" Yes, my good woman, it indeed is a subtle sweetener, most calming to
the constitution. Have you a boy, haply, who might precede me with it to the
king's chamber? I would not let it out of my sight, for fear of accidents."

" Aye, sir, I bet there be a plenty hanging round ready to filch some'at
when one's back's turned.—Here, Tom—Sid—one o' you lubbers; make your-
self a bit spruce off to the pump.—He'll be back 'fore a flea jumps, your
worship."

The upper hall, weakly illumined with tallow dips; a gallery across its
further end, to which leads a stairway on the left; on the right a huge hearth
with its piled unlit logs; stray gleams twinkle like stars from false eyes, jetty
claws, or shiny teeth all round; a long table runs under the gallery loaded
with viands; servants move to and fro.

While, at the near end of the hall, under windows against which rain
rattles, talk, almost lost in shadows, a group of courtiers.

" I say she's a witch."

" Nay, nay, for she's my sister."

" I beg your highness's pardon, but I think you must admit there's excuse."

" Well, may be so."

"I hope that your highness would not take it ill, should she die
suddenly?"

" No, my fondness could bear the strain."

" Master Fustian is barely descended to the kitchen, so if you'd rather—"

" No, she is a traitor; for any who intercepts the authority of a sovereign
is such."

" What I'm afraid of is, frankly, her tricks."

" I fear failure."

" Failure, pooh! barely possible, so far as I see."

" But look, here comes Master Fustian with the dish."

" There!"

" Bah! what a clumsy clown! he's got stumbling at the first step."

" Up they go."

Along the gallery light shines, and the king's daughter walks.

The boy stumbles and falls back on Master Fustian; they finish the descent
together. Master Fustian, spitting all over the floor,—

" Gracious me! I believe—Oh! have pity, pity, my God! I think I have
got some of it on my lips, my tongue. Oh! I'm lost, as good as dead!
Poisoned! Arsenic!"

Confusion.

In which enters from a side door the prince's pretty wife and her maidens.

Her he had married and a bad temper; he rather would have had her
alone, but could in no way help himself.

21

That night, getting her tantrums, she broke from its gold mount the coral branch which stood on the dressing-table for her rings to hang on : caught her foot in the new silver-embroidered bed-testers, tearing loose half a dozen yards ; flounced about ; stamped her feet so hard she hurt them ; then cried, and said it was his fault ; at last said she would not have him in bed with her, and with an " I hate you " bade him crawl under.

Which he, though brave enough on horseback, began to do.

When a draught blew open the half-latched door, and a light shone in ; outside there walked the king's lonely daughter.

The prince scrambled out and slammed the door ; nevertheless, seemingly, the tantrums had found time to escape, for his wife said no more about going under the bed.

If on getting in he was pinched black and blue, as she had threatened, he made no one wiser about it.

Gusts teased the jolly trees till, wrathful, they cursed ; the sky, black and rugged as an old tarred barge-bottom, took a rusty glow of resentment from the torches ; all the folk stood shivering round the Home of Comfort.

The prince advances towards a great pile of combustibles heaped against the walls, a torch in his hand.

Flames leap, roar, and flare up into the sky ; but the spiteful wind drives them over, not on the castle but on the crowd, scattering it on all sides.

They would, in another instant, have caught autumn-dried hedge and tree, and have stretched devastating away over the country. But the king's daughter's taper gleams out of the great hall-window where she walks ; at the same instant the flames gobble one another up, and die away like fire-works.

Then a voice roared out from the interior, as from a giant's huge chest—
" Both hale and well and blithe and bland
I live when no one cares for me :
But he that would close grasp my hand
A dwindling death is sure to see.
But I'm King Comfort after all ;
Sins I can pardon great and small,
And need none handy to my call
Save my dear daughter, Privacy."

T. Sturge Moore.

So I AM COME INTO MY GARDEN *So* MY SISTER *So* *my* SPOUSE *So*
So   *So*   *So*
O BELOVED.

The
Shula-
mite.

I SLEEP, BUT MY
HEART WAKETH:
it is THE VOICE
OF MY BELOVED THAT
KNOCKETH, *saying*, OP-
EN TO ME, MY SISTER,
MY LOVE, MY DOVE, MY
UNDEFILED: FOR MY
HEAD IS FILLED WITH
DEW, *and* MY LOCKS
WITH THE DROPS OF
THE NIGHT.

CHAP V

HEART'S DEMESNE.

Listen, bright lady, thy deep pansie eyes
Made never answer when my eyes did pray,
Than with those quaintest looks of blank surprise,

But my love-longing has devised a way
To mock thy living image, from thy hair
To thy rose toes, and keep thee by alway.

My garden's face is o l so maidly fair,
With limbs all tapering, and with hues all fresh ;
Thine are the beauties all that flourish there.

Amaranth, fadeless, tells me of thy flesh ;
Briar-rose knows thy cheek ; the Pink thy pout ;
Bunched kisses dangle from the Woodbine mesh.

I love to loll, when Daisy stars peep out,
To hear the music of my garden dell,
Hollyhock's laughter, and the Sunflower's shout,

And many whisper things I dare not tell.

JOHN GRAY.

23

LES DEMOISELLES DE SAUVE.

Beautiful ladies through the orchard pass ;
Bend under crutched-up branches, forked and low,
Trailing their samet palls o'er dew-drenched grass.

Pale blossoms, looking on proud Jacqueline,
Blush to the colour of her finger tips,
And rosy knuckles, laced with yellow lace.

High-crested Berthe discerns, with slant, clinched eyes,
Amid the leaves, pink faces of the skies :
She locks her plaintive hands Sainte-Margot-wise.

Ysabeau follows last with languorous pace ;
Presses, voluptuous, to her bursting lips,
With backward stoop, a bunch of eglantine.

Courtly ladies through the orchard pass ;
Bow low, as in lords' halls, and springtime grass
Tangles a snare to catch the tapering toe.

JOHN GRAY.

THE accusation was brought against our first Dial of mere art eclecticism ; one thing, keenly attractive to us, might explain this reprehensible selectiveness, a little thing we think common to all good art. Inseparable from the garment of individuality, the word *Document* perfectly explains this.

Record of some remembered delight, record perhaps of a mere moment in transfigured life, producing and controlling it, the word *Document* represents some exquisite detail in a masterpiece, convincing to the spectator as a thing known, yet not of necessity the symbol of borrowed story—possibly, there, the mere symbol of time.   A thing easily imagined away from a picture, but authoritative there, as a gesture, or poetical recollection, the lattice-light cast upon the wall in Rossetti's " Proserpine," the azalea near the scattered hair in Whistler's " White Harmony, number three," might be chosen to prove that *Document* is not necessarily the mere machinery giving vraisemblance to positive subject, for these pictures are almost without it.

Rossetti, it is true, adds to his work a sonnet, and between this and the picture some delicate interchime penetrates the sense with a conviction in its symbol, adding meaning to the well-like light ; to the fatality that seems to brood about the shadows ; to this face that listens to the ebb and flow of footsteps hastening.   The fateful pomegranate might, however, be put into the hand of many an Italian portrait, the title *Donna Innominata* painted

25

on the frame would not destroy this picture's memorableness—to-morrow the name Proserpine might be given to Da Vinci's Monna Lisa, and so, seemingly, unseal its secret. In Whistler's "White Harmony" the subject is intentionally fugitive,—a chosen place where ladies live, with something of the pale life of lilies listening to the music of their shapes. Yet in this secret air that drowses over the perfume of hair and flower, and penetrating, as it were, this mute harmony, some stray notes would convey undertone-symbol, preexistence, and chime about the picture faintly, like evening music echoed by a river.

These works have been chosen for their lack of story, in its common acceptance ; and so we come easily to the colour exclamation on some Chinese enamel, dabbed there in vibrant crimson on a liquid purple, where no subject can exist at all ; yet this thing, by its cunning spontaneity, will give the emotion that sudden movement adds to nature—the ripple of grass in a summer landscape for instance—and so become *Document*—that monument of moods. A viol left on a lowering bough by some singer who has ceased, one marigold drowned in a space of water, would convey, within a picture and without, this sense of existence and preexistence, this sense of time.

In the work of the English Pre-Raphaelites, document has been chiselled in new-cleft gems ; in Impressionism, it has been wrapped in strokes that waved into air, or that palpitated into light ; far be it then from us to claim it treasure trove, for we think it inseparable from all art excellence—capable even of being spun to the veriest gossamer thread of definition. More common thirty years ago than at present, it may appear unfamiliar, its recentness has made it obsolete and strange.

We make no claim to originality, not feeling wiser than did Solomon who doubtless wrote the Song of Songs ; for all art is but the combination of known quantities, the interplay of a few senses only ; that some spirit seems to transfuse these, is due to a cunning use of a sixth sense—the sense of possible relation commonly called Soul, probably a second sense of touch more subtle than the first—and this sense is more common to the craftsman used to self-control than habit would allow.

We would therefore avoid all taint of announced reform for those pathetically persistent in demanding it ; dawn itself promises day only to some, not to all ; and Art has been, Art is, this is the pledge that it will be again.

"Fresh with some colour, a cloud breaks upon the sky. Dawn grows, wanes, and stretches fibres of frail light ; this is the signal to white hazy moths to shimmer above the gummy vines ; and stagnant water grows steel-like and hard.

"Suddenly the cock crows ; he is awake ; long before, he has mistaken one or two accidents in the night for signals that he should announce the light, his accuracy in utterance is merely sentimental."

One word more of apology.

All past effort has seemed more conscious of aim, more direct, than it was really ; we imagine an effort towards renaissance, springing from a white hand beckoning above the ashes of some forgotten city, and seen at some time by one in whom the possible germ of a new art was placed. Again, revelation has come to one reading a book, or to one who fancies he has seen a grey torso beneath a cliff in some forgotten creek, and that it rocked with the water's motion. We forget those previous years, wasted in barren yearning, satisfied at last by something contemporary ; imitation following, too often without knowledge of the new result attained.

To-day the announcement that you believe in Nature, or in *Ideas*, affords claim to originality, and we would avoid this announcement. By the word Idea is meant, that formulated experience of the many, their guarantee in life against future failure. Strange, this flattery of common thought, this useless pandering to the crowd, incapable in its appreciation to surpass the annual shilling or two, for some exhibition ; for its characteristic is peevish lassitude—the bankruptcy of disinterest ; the reviews have long since assured it as to contemporary lack of originality, separating this work from that master, to attribute it to his wife.

Indifference is only crested at times by little exasperated words, frost-bitten fronds, crooked and meaningless : let admiration be one of the reasons for the Dial to exist ; admiration, so often fruitful of self-respect, nay more, it is "the essence of all art "—it is that which makes us wish in childhood, when power is not yet, and before experience has shut the gates, for larger flowers, something that would prevent soft, gentle beasts from walking away, the growth of berried twigs so out of reach, for these are the first stray waifs of all art feeling. Let the great artists yet alive be witness that copybook culture is the only reason for this colourless currency in art and thought ; the rainbow of Art is still there for Hope to look through, all pleasantness has not been snatched from the meadows and hills of Nature's royalty, Art has been, Art is, so the present touches wings with the past.

" In the naïf delight and fantastic objectiveness we call primitive art feeling, space was found for the august and reticent personality of Piero della Francesca ; his work was sweet besides with occasional convolvulus tendril, or nestling finch, gay in some trick of dress revealing personality, some shapely gem or crown of selected leaf. Giorgione painted the Greek Theseus —but as St. George naked in a brook, his work fulfilled. Since then the world would expect *this* development with the budding of the garden peas, *that* quality with the bursting of the pod. Experience would, for convenience, separate the quality of form from its blossoming into colour, little caring to note its oneness—for in continuance from environing space, to the central surfaces, Form, Greek Form, as it is called, is colour ; colour is continued line ; without it, form is but some personal conviction not visual at all, a mental building into air, a reasoned spanning of given space. Change, with its contradiction, its return to the past, appears again in Romantic Art, which, nevertheless, would control Art and Nature more than did the older styles ; dominate it by individuality at high vibrant pitch—Nature strained into symbolic action, and in an atmosphere dyed by personal feeling.—Slowly

27

the old fantastic details of primitive art return, with these, the old ornamental-
ness ; lyrical movement recoils, becomes arrested, a tense immobility ensues,
more ultimate than the great calm of the Antique, for upon the Parthenon,
the great divine limbs leap and rebound, the draperies cling close to flesh,
deep with the possibility of sweat."

1 THE BRIDAL 2 ELLA THE SHE-BEAR

1

"HOW SEEMETH, HOW SEEMETH
OUR ANNA MITREVNA?"

2

"THIS IS NOT A SAVAGE BEAR;
IT IS ELKA, THE SHE-DRAGON."

I

THE ground-mist folds round the green earth in a robe that is grey below, but rose against the sky, circling tree-tops as a sea circles islands; the tree-tops look wan. Rises the sun refreshed like a bridegroom; Mother Earth shivers through her veils, like a bride; the hills sigh softly; hedge-flowers gleam with a whiteness of morning stars, raising tiny cups, tiny crowns, all, save those that muse till it is day.

Now the high roads echo, echo loudly, with brisk footfalls, gay talking, and much laughter; each maiden, in a green or new red kirtle, each beautiful damsel, is bright with ribands and neatly braided hair. Fine young fellows, on swift horses, ride up from the cross-roads, with greetings to the chatting parents, brightest glances for the daughters, and they ask—"Where is this feast and beautiful betrothal of Anna Mitrevna, the fair Anna Mitrevna, to that powerful lord Ivan Timofeievich?"—and all give prompt answer, with hands raised forward to sweep the horizon, "There! there is no bidding, all are welcome; and, oh! how merry will be this merry wedding, and glad with many people; so bide with us, as we are going there."

Fresh grass becomes trodden by hastening feet; the morning air tingles to the sound of gay guslas; the White House gleams in dew-dipped sunlight; about jump happy people, with heavy feet they jump in circles, thumping the ground, they dance with outstretched arms, singing—"Oh! singing ha, and ha, this merry wedding!"

"*Come, come, bright sun!*
Come forth, good people!
I have caught Katenka, Katenka,
In my cornfield, nigh the oak-grove,
Katenka, to be my bride."

Within the house, fair Anna Mitrevna sits among the tire-maidens. They have washed her white limbs, they have robed them in silk, and combed her pale thin hair with a silver comb, they have braided her hair till it hangs below her girdle, the girdle is of silk well spun: in a diadem of gold, she sits among the maidens; they laugh softly, but she does not laugh; her mother has fallen on her neck and passionately kissed her, yet she could not weep.

29

Anna Mitrevna is tall, slender as a Rousalka, her face is white, her eyes are like hawk's eyes, and she sits among the maidens.

Lord Ivan has come, with all his kinsmen, to woo, to seek the damsel ; he asks of some of her near companions, "How seemeth, but how seemeth, our Anna Mitrevna ?" and they chant and sing the bridal song, and answer him, that she is tall, and very slender, as a Rousalka, her hair is plaited to her waist,—golden the hair, but light beneath the golden crown—and her eyes are like a hawk's.

Anna's portly father donned a flowered robe and called loudly to his daughter, whilst hired singers carol a merry song ; yet the bridegroom waits.

Her mother has folded in stately folds the wedding veil ; but the bride does not move.

Ivan's father has taken her by the hand, her parents push gently at her shoulders : they leave the room, the outer threshold, where waits the noble wooer looking handsome. His mantle is of marten's skin, his curly head bonny with a scarlet cap, trimmed about with silver ; thus he stands before the hazel-coppice.

> " *You, you can not hold me,*
> *Yet you would kiss me,*
> *Boris, with your lips, Boris !*
> *Yours pout like a grey mushroom,*
> *Mine laugh like a rose.*"

But, faltering, she grapples with his sturdy shoulders, cries in his face "Thou red-eyed devil ! cruel devil ! ah ! with those red eyes ! red with blood ! also thy hands, that most treacherously slew Vladimir Kamarazin, my comely, my beloved lover ! "

She tears the dagger from his belt, thrusts it in his breadth of breast, holding on with both hands till his cruel heart is pierced, and with gaze revulsed he falls to the damp earth for a bridal-bed, a dead bride by his side upon the chilly ground, for his brothers have slain her.

The red sun sets behind the forest, now it is time for her soul to depart, departing thus it addresses the sinful body and bitterly laments :

"Farewell ! farewell ! oh thou, my white body! poor body! thou hast felt but little joy, yet so much sorrow ; thou goest, sinful body, to the cold earth to be devoured, to be dissolved.—There lies Vladimir Kamarazin. I cannot dissolve, or lie in the still ground with Vladimir Kamazarin ! for I, the soul, must go to grief eternal, to a terrible, an eternal agony."

2 ELLA THE SHE-BEAR.

> " Since thou hast parted from thy mother
> Thou art a pale yellow,
> Like a yellow orange,
> And like a green bush."

How snug was the bears' house in winter : it was pleasant to listen to the tinkle of the falling snow as it crept without, or cunningly clomb the pine-trunks, to get back to Mother Sky ; but the bears' house was pleasanter in summer, for about it a cool black pine-wood hummed and talked, broad fragrant boughs drooped above the door; yet, in a damp cave, some few rocks beyond the thinning of the trees, lived the She-Dragon Elka, the White Enchantress who loved beautiful men, but doted most upon young husbands. She was wicked and subtle, so many mothers had she made to mourn, in the hamlets through the absence of lovers the gardens drooped, and the graves blossomed. Bridal sheets, well spun with loud singing, remained unbleached, for the brooks were full of tears. Prowling at night in the shape of a She-Bear, she called the youthful shepherds "sweetheart," and by her cunning enchantments seemed to them a white woman ; tall as a green palm, softer than driven snow, white cream, or the sprinkling of the plum in blossom ; when they had tasted of her treacherous lips, they grew very wan and yellow ; as bushes do in autumn, they faded away. But to those Elka did not love she seemed a grey She-Bear ; and the bears hated her, gladly they would have killed her, but how could they? They bitterly cursed her when she was not near ; mother-bears were troubled if the father spake of her doings, and they would have slain her, but they dared not.

One Saturday, the little Ella heard these things, as her mother combed her fur; the little She-Bear seemed as though she did not listen, yet her honied eyes flashed, like sungleams caught in cruel icicles ; she shut them that she might the better remember, and thought " it would be very pleasant to be an enchantress, seemingly like a soft woman, with a face like a blossoming tree, soft as the drift of the blossoming plum, and to love beautiful men."

Came the young spring coyly as a betrothed—like a bride, with nosegays upon her green kirtle—and she whispered to the black pines who laughed into light buds : running among the trees she filled them with scents and airs, the banks with soft strawberries and furry mosses. When the tender corn skipped from the ground the very rills sang like birds. Ella's desire burst from bud into blossom, her coat shone like silk, with a lovesong in each ear, she has left her mother ; to each stranger she has said, " I am Elka the White Dragon."

Malemka, Sirma, Daria, sweet maidens all, washed winding-sheets in the brook, Irma made poppy-cakes. Each sister was stripped to the waist, the men being away, all save the dead man their brother ; as they washed the winding-cloths, with the flow of the waters they wept.

When they saw Ella they started and fled, so left the linen, to float down the stream to the eddies, past the mill, to the eddies, to the bridge, where the little children said, " Look! look! at the drowned white woman in the stream."

Young Ella wondered at her wisdom, her spells, for he was of great beauty, the shepherd Stoyan, and stalwart as he lay on the couch, but a faded lily his face—his eyes she could not see, for, as the bud hides the honey-drop, his eyelids hid his glance ; he slept.

Ella's heart throbbed like a cuckoo's song, she whispered softly, " 'Tis I, 'tis I, my dear love! dear love, why dost thou hide thine eyes from me? 'tis I, yes I, thine Elka, thy loving enchantress."

Now the men have left the pits, and some the kilns, or the hewing of wood ; they droop their heads like grass, their hands like falling leaves, for their sisters and sisters-in-law have told them how the cruel Elka is with poor Stoyan, Stoyan who has died of her many enchantments, "and we left the winding-sheets to float down the river ;"

"A bird flew away with a poppy-cake, and with it my heart fled away."

Then all longed to kill the enchantress, but they dared not, they wished to slay her, but how could they? Yet a priest who was old, comforted them, saying :

"Rather let us rejoice, that God, in his goodness, has delivered her into our hands, for mark ye, good people, that it is day, and not night, for it is noon ; let each man take him a cudgel, and let Michel, the son of Nicholas, toll the bell, that warns the people of the passing of spirits, perchance this spirit is but some stray Lamia not clothed by the night."

Poor, poor foolish Ella half died with fear when came the pealing and rolling of the bell ; she shook and moaned, and would have entreated the enchantress, but she dared not ; gladly would she have fled, but how could she ? she crept crying to the door, where Basil, the stalwart woodman, struck her with his axe, and all the brave young fellows beat her into a thousand pieces.

3 SNOW IN SPRING.

"The streams gush from the heart of the earth,
The earth as she sorrows.
If the sun knew half the sorrow of the earth,
The earth in sorrow,
The sun would turn pale and hollow, like the Moon."

The Sister. The apple-bloom like snow tinged with blood drifts to the earth, my brother, my red sun, do not go away, this is snow in spring.

The Brother. Do not weep for me, my sister, do not sob like a labouring brook, snow melts in water, your tears will not melt this snow ; the apple-bloom in spring is ever flecked with blood, for the earth and pine-roots crave for blood in spring, till the Infidel be driven away ; and, oh my flower-sister ! the little brooks will wash my body of its sins, each eye they will wash clean as a separate crystal, that my eyes may forget. The tree-roots will comb my hair ; the earth kiss and wrap each limb of mine ; for if I die, will not the birds bury the hero, the willow and elder sing me to sleep? and the purple anemones, that are the eyes of the field, will watch above my grave.

The Sister. Brother! brother! didst thou not hear the sobbing of the wood-pigeons to the pines ? the pigeons that have stolen their murmurs from the brooks. The pine-trunks reel red, drunk with blood :—Oh, my brother ! the oak-trees tell me that in spring the gallows-tree grows in Priapol for the merriment of the governor's wife, the governor's children : for those whose grave is not already red in the woods, the gallows puts on boughs.

And behold, as he went by the high roads, the birds, the trees, the rivers, and the little brooks said to him "do not go," and the apple-trees said " this is snow in spring; the wasting of thy fruit; thou art snow in spring, through thee a maiden's womb shall swell with nought but barren longing." And the rivers said "We shall wash thee of all thy blood, wash thee, so will the rains." And the tree-roots crept nearer, "We shall comb thy hair with our grey fingers, the birds and the winds will bury thee with leaves that did not live." Then the black earth said, "I shall rock thee in my lap, bind thee with night, and kiss thy lips that thou mayest never see, or remember, whilst the willow and elder will sing thee to sleep."

When he, the hero, had met the *wanderer* on the spot near the road, where the trees grow thinly, the elder-tree said to the dead man, "Lo! I and the willow sing thee to sleep, were we not right? thou frost in spring!" but he smiled at their song. The earth, wrapping him round, said, "I was right!" yet he opened not his mouth, and the birds told the rivers, and the rivers complained.

But he laughed, because he knew they could not mean what they said. CHARLES RICKETTS.

☞ WE WOULD THANK
TSM. & HJR.
WHOSE TIMELY AID
MADE POSSIBLE THE
PUBLICATION OF THIS
NUMBER OF THE DIAL.

THE DIAL ❧ NO 2 ❧
OF THE SERIES.

*The cover and decorations in the
text, have been designed and engraved
on the wood by . . . Charles Ricketts*

ꝫ ꝫ CONTENTS ꝫ ꝫ
ꝫ   ꝫ   ꝫ

*The issue is strictly limited
to two hundred copies, numbered,
of which this is* . .

Nº 129

THE VALE
1892

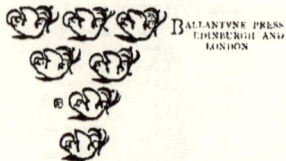
BALLANTYNE PRESS
EDINBURGH AND
LONDON

1892

www.ingramcontent.com/pod-product-compliance
Lightning Source LLC
Chambersburg PA
CBHW022029080426
42733CB00007B/776